MINIMUS SECUNDUS

Moving on in Latin

Barbara Bell

Joint Association of Classical Teachers

Illustrations by **Helen Forte**

CAMBRIDGE
UNIVERSITY PRESS

PUBLISHED BY THE PRESS SYNDICATE OF THE UNIVERSITY OF CAMBRIDGE
The Pitt Building, Trumpington Street, Cambridge, United Kingdom

CAMBRIDGE UNIVERSITY PRESS
The Edinburgh Building, Cambridge CB2 2RU, UK
40 West 20th Street, New York, NY 10011–4211, USA
477 Williamstown Road, Port Melbourne, VIC 3207, Australia
Ruiz de Alarcón 13, 28014 Madrid, Spain
Dock House, The Waterfront, Cape Town 8001, South Africa

http://www.cambridge.org

First published 2004

Printed in the United Kingdom at the University Press, Cambridge

Typeface Macra Palatino 12/14pt   *System* QuarkXPress®

A catalogue record for this book is available from the British Library

ISBN 0 521 75545 X   paperback

Produced by Kamae Design, Oxford
Design by Angela Ashton
Illustrations by Helen Forte
Cover illustration by Helen Forte

ACKNOWLEDGEMENTS
The author is indebted to many individuals who have helped with *Minimus secundus* in a variety of ways: to Lindsay Allason–Jones, Elizabeth Hartley, Patrick Ottaway and Jeremy Paterson for research into Roman York; to the Birley family and all at Vindolanda for help with the early chapters; to Niall Rudd for corrections to the Latin; to Rachel Wood for countless improvements to the text and lay-out; to the many teachers who took part in the testing programme and who provided feedback and encouragement, especially Oliver Makower and Peter Jones, who provided constant support.

The creativity, imagination and support of my Advisory Panel transformed the text; my deep thanks to Jean Cross, Helen Forte, Wendy Hunt, Pam Macklin, Dawn Perry, Brian Sparkes, Diana Sparkes and Tim Wheeler. Adriana Goldenberg advised on the Romanian language.

My best thanks are owed to Nick, Joanna and Kate, who have stuck by me as *minimus* has become *maximus*.

Thanks are due to the following for permission to reproduce photographs: p.9, The Vindolanda Trust; p.16, The British Museum; p.33, p.47, York Archaeological Trust for Excavation and Research Ltd; p.37, p.82, Yorkshire Museum; p.53, The Art Archive/Museo della Civilta Romana Rome/Dagli Orti; p.54, p.62, p.66, The Bridgeman Art Library, London; p.70, The Bridgeman Art Library, London/Museo Archeologico, Florence, Italy; p.79, Dean & Chapter of York; p.89*t*, Museum of Antiquities of the University and Society of Antiquaries of Newcastle upon Tyne; p.89*b*, Tulles House Museum, Carlisle.

CONTENTS

Introduction

The family you will meet in this book has been living at Vindolanda, a Roman fort in the north of Britain. They are not originally from Rome, but from Batavia (the Netherlands). Flavius, the father, joined the Roman army and his whole family travelled across the sea to Vindolanda to join him. Here they are:

Flavius, aged 45, is in charge of the fort	His wife, Lepidina, aged 37	Flavia, their daughter, aged 21
Iulius, their elder son, aged 18	Rufus, their younger son, aged 8	Corinthus, their educated Greek slave, aged 47
Candidus, their skilled Celtic slave, aged 41	Pandora, Lepidina's slave girl, aged 31	Their cat, Vibrissa, who is always chasing mice . . .

. . . and I'm their mouse, Minimus!

It is the year AD 105. We are leaving Vindolanda this summer because Flavius has a new job in Eboracum (York). It's a very long journey so we will need to stop on the way. I've never travelled before – I hope I won't get lost! I suppose Vibrissa will be coming too . . . **ēheu!**

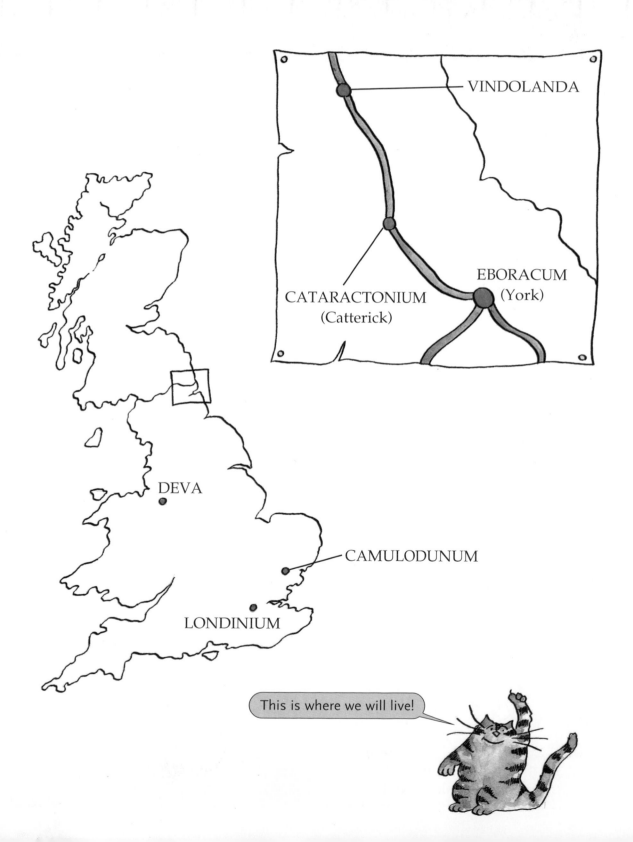

VINDOLANDA

CATARACTONIUM
(Catterick)

EBORACUM
(York)

DEVA

CAMULODUNUM

LONDINIUM

This is where we will live!

1 Iūlius
Last days at Vindolanda

A special occasion

Now that Flavius is leaving Vindolanda, all the soldiers are taking part in a big parade: they are saying goodbye to him and to his family.

1. pompa appropinquat. pompa magnifica est!

ita vērō!

Lepidīna et Iūlius pompam spectant.

2. Rūfe! equum spectā!

equus splendidus est. euge!

Pandōra Rūfum vocat.

3. ecce! pater equitat.

ita vērō. equus praecipuus est!

Rūfus Corinthum vocat.

4. Candide! Flāvius equitat.

equus magnificus est!

Corinthus Candidum vocat.

5. mīlitēs appropinquant.
aliī incēdunt, aliī equitant.

6. euge! Flāvius praefectus optimus est!

7 Minimus et Vibrissa dormiunt.

8 subitō clāmōrem audiunt.

c-c-cūr omnēs agitātī sunt?

tum Rūfus rem explicat.

9 euge! laetī sumus!

Minimus pompam spectat.
Vibrissa Minimum spectat.

10 valē! grātiās tibi agimus!

WORDS TO HELP

Nouns

clāmōrem noise
pompa parade
praefectus commander

Verbs

appropinquat it approaches/is approaching
audiunt they hear/are hearing
equitat he rides/is riding
incēdunt they march/are marching

Adjectives

agitātī excited
laetī happy
omnēs all, everyone
praecipuus special

Adverbs

subitō suddenly
tum then

Exclamations

ecce! look!
euge! hooray!
valē! goodbye!

Idioms

aliī . . . aliī . . . some . . . others . . .
ita vērō yes
rem explicat explains the situation

Question word

cūr? why?

GRASP THE GRAMMAR

The most important word in a sentence is the **verb**; it describes what **action** is happening. In Latin, the verb is normally found at the **end** of the sentence.

Look carefully at these two sentences. Can you remember what they mean?

a Minimus pompam **spectat**.
b Lepidīna et Iūlius pompam **spectant**.

In each sentence, the verb is in **bold**. Notice that **spectat** means "he watches/ he is watching" but **spectant** means "they watch/they are watching". **Latin uses different verb endings to show** *who* **is doing the action**.

Notice too that there is no word for "he" or "they". The ending of the verb shows us who is doing the watching.

Here is the full set of six verb endings:

spectō	I watch/am watching	spectāmus	we watch/are watching
spectās	you watch/are watching*	spectātis	you watch/are watching**
spectat	he/she/it watches/is watching	spectant	they watch/are watching

* when "you" refers to one person (**singular**)
** when "you" refers to more than one person (**plural**)

We call this set of endings the **present** tense, because the action is happening **now**.

Here are some more **verbs**. Translate them into English, taking care to check the endings to see *who* is doing the action:

1 equitat

2 appropinquant

3 vocō

4 equitāmus

5 spectat

6 equitō

7 appropinquātis

8 spectātis

9 equitant

10 vocās

11 spectāmus

12 appropinquās

Try to remember those endings because then you can understand hundreds of Latin verbs!

But here's one verb that is a bit different!

From the pictures on pages 6 and 7, try to work out the meaning of **est**, **sumus** and **sunt**.

These are all parts of the verb "to be". This verb needs special care: it doesn't follow the normal pattern for verbs in Latin – or in any other language in fact! It's called an **irregular** verb.

sum	I am	**sumus**	we are
es	you are	**estis**	you are
est	he/she/it is	**sunt**	they are

LATIN ROOTS

Use your knowledge of Latin to explain the underlined word in each sentence.

1 The Queen likes to watch <u>equestrian</u> events.
2 If you are a singer, you must look after your <u>vocal</u> cords.
3 Most football clubs now provide seating for the <u>spectators</u>.
4 In some countries, young people still do a period of <u>military</u> service.
5 Vesuvius is a <u>dormant</u> volcano.
6 Teachers sometimes use <u>audio-visual</u> aids in lessons.

ROMAN REPORT

Uncovering the past

Flavius and his family lived at Vindolanda for about six years at the beginning of the second century AD. Trying to piece together all the evidence for their life there is rather like doing a large jigsaw puzzle.

■ Archaeologists who have excavated at Vindolanda can tell us a lot about this family. They have found many interesting items that belonged to the family and to other people who lived inside and outside the Roman fort. For example, we can see Lepidina's sandals, her comb in its case and her sewing needles. These **artefacts** are displayed in the Chesterholm museum at Vindolanda.

■ Every year, archaeologists dig at Vindolanda. They have found the remains of **buildings** used by the soldiers and by Flavius and his family. They have worked out the size of these buildings, including the actual house that the family lived in.

■ When the family left the fort, Flavius decided to burn his personal **letters** along with the records of the fort. However, the wooden writing tablets were not completely destroyed. They were buried and when archaeologists excavated them they were able to read the messages.

This is the type of decorative head-dress which was worn by Flavius's horse in the parade

■ Archaeologists have also found altars and tombstones that have **inscriptions** on them. These give us valuable information about the people who lived in the fort and about their religious beliefs.

An important job

After the parade, Flavius gives the soldiers some surprising orders.

WORDS TO HELP

Nouns

ancillae slave girls
lāridum lard
ligna logs
rogum bonfire
silicēs flints
silvam forest
tabulās writing tablets

Verbs

ardet it burns/is burning
colligite! collect
currunt they run/are running
facimus we do/are doing
fundunt they pour/are pouring
iactant they throw/are throwing
nescio I don't know
terunt they rub/are rubbing
truncant they cut/are cutting

Pronoun

hoc this

Adjective

calidum hot

GRASP THE GRAMMAR

A **noun** is the name of a person, a place or a thing. Names of people and places are called **proper nouns**. They always have a capital letter, both in English and in Latin, for example Pandora, Rufus and Vindolanda.
All other words in Latin begin with a small letter.

Nouns can do different jobs in a sentence. The person or thing *doing the action* is called the **subject** of the sentence; the person or thing *having the action done to them* is called the **object**. In Latin, nouns that are the **object** of a sentence have different endings.

Look at these two sentences:

a rogus ardet.   The bonfire is burning.
b mīlitēs rogum cōnstruunt.   The soldiers build a bonfire.

In sentence **a**, the bonfire is the **subject**. In sentence **b**, it is the **object**, so it changes from **rogus** to **rogum**.

Copy out these sentences and translate them into English. Then underline the verb, both in English and in Latin. Finally, put an **s** over the **subject** and an **o** over the object. The first one is done for you.

```
        s        o              s          o
```
1 Pandōra Rūfum <u>vocat</u>. = Pandora <u>calls</u> Rufus.
2 Lepidīna pompam spectat.
3 Minimus clāmōrem audit.
4 Iūlius rem explicat.
5 Vibrissa Minimum spectat.
6 omnēs flammās spectant.
7 mīlitēs tabulās iactant.

Pandora decides to tell Rufus a story to cheer him up. He loved the parade with the wonderful horse so she tells him the story of another special horse.

PEGASUS THE WONDER-HORSE

Long ago in Greece there lived a handsome hero called Bellerophon. He quarrelled with Proteus, the King of Corinth, so the King gave him some terrible tasks to do. One of these was to kill a monster called the Chimaera, a strange beast which breathed fire. It had the head of a lion, the body of a goat and a snake for a tail. It was destroying the land. Bellerophon went to sleep, wondering how he could kill such a frightening creature. While he slept, the goddess Minerva appeared and left a golden bridle by his side. When he woke up, Bellerophon saw a wonderful horse with wings. This horse was called Pegasus. With the help of the golden bridle, he mounted the horse and soared into the sky in search of the Chimaera. Once he caught sight of it he swooped down low, choked its fiery breath with lead and cut its head off. Bellerophon was so proud of his achievements that he decided to fly Pegasus up to Mount Olympus, where the gods lived. Jupiter was angry with Bellerophon for his arrogance so he sent a gadfly to sting Pegasus. Bellerophon was thrown from his horse and plummeted to earth.

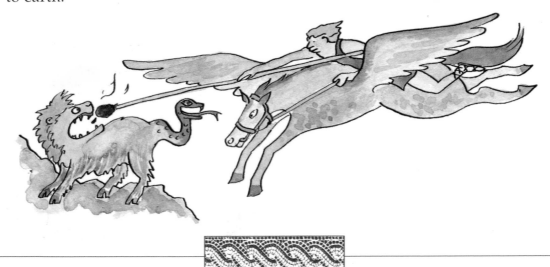

Remember, the **verb** is the action word in the sentence!

And a **noun** is the name of a person, a place or a thing.

A soldier at last!

Iulius has joined the Roman army and will soon be leaving Vindolanda.
He discusses this plan with Flavius and Rufus.

 ## WORDS TO HELP

Nouns

bellum war
dea goddess
imperātor emperor
iter journey
mare sea
pontem bridge

Verbs

aedificant they build
nōlī timēre! don't be afraid!
superant they win
vādō I go

Adjectives

nōtissimae very famous
perīculōsum dangerous
sollicitus worried

Question words

quid? what?
quis? who?
ubi? where?

Adverbs

ibi there
scīlicet of course
semper always
tam so

Conjunctions

quod because
quoque also
sed but

Idiom

bellum gerit he is
  fighting a war

Prepositions

prope near
trāns across

GRASP THE GRAMMAR

In chapter 1 you learnt that a noun is a naming word for a person, a place or a thing. Nouns can be *described* by words known as **adjectives**.

Latin nouns are said to be **masculine**, **feminine** or **neuter**. ("Neuter" means neither masculine nor feminine.) This is called the **gender** of the noun.

Whenever we use an adjective to describe a noun, it must be the same **gender** as the noun. For example, Rufus is **sollicit<u>us</u>** (masculine) but Lepidina would be **sollicit<u>a</u>** (feminine).

Look at the four sentences below. In each sentence there is one **noun** and in each case it is described by one **adjective**.

Copy out each sentence in Latin and then write down what it means in English. In each sentence, underline the **noun** and the **adjective**. Then write the letter **n** above the noun and the letter **a** above the adjective.

1 legiōnēs nōtissimae sunt.
2 mīlitēs Rōmānī semper superant.
3 Lepidīna laeta nōn est.
4 bellum perīculōsum est.

> Remember, the only nouns that have a capital letter in Latin are the names of people or places – **proper** nouns.

> How observant are you? In Latin, does the **adjective** normally come before or after the **noun**?

> To help you understand the idea of the **gender** of a noun, we'll mark it in "Words to help" from now on. Look out for **m** (= masculine), **f** (= feminine) and **n** (= neuter). We'll give the masculine, feminine and neuter forms of adjectives too.

 LATIN ROOTS

Use your knowledge of Latin to explain the underlined word in each sentence.

1 If a striker scores the winning goal in a cup final, he will achieve <u>notable</u> success.
2 I hope to play the <u>principal</u> boy in next year's pantomime.
3 The boats will be moored in the <u>marina</u> during the summer.
4 It is <u>perilous</u> to walk along the edge of a roof.
5 You may feel rather <u>timid</u> when you start a new school.
6 You need to take a <u>transatlantic</u> flight to go to the United States.

> Did you get the last one right? Now have a competition: see how many words you can find in English which begin with "trans-". All these words come from Latin. If you're stuck, use your dictionary!

ROMAN REPORT

Joining up

Iulius is eighteen and he is about to join the Roman army. Before being accepted, he has to pass a fitness test and promise that he will be loyal to the Roman emperor. Since his father Flavius is prefect of the camp, Iulius will join the army as an officer, called a **tribune**. He will join a legion called II Traiana. This is a new legion, assembled by the emperor Trajan specially for the wars in Dacia. (Today this country is called Romania.)

Check the evidence

When we want to find out about a Roman emperor (what he did, what he looked like, what sort of person he was) we need to check the evidence carefully. Sometimes we have archaeological remains that show what the emperor built, for example Hadrian's Wall in the north of Britain. Sometimes we have accounts by ancient writers that tell us about his character, for example Suetonius wrote a work called *Lives of the Emperors*. Sometimes we have coins and statues that show what the emperor looked like. In the case of Trajan, we can see Trajan's forum in Rome and the column that was built in his honour to show his victories in Dacia. We also have several written accounts of his character and achievements.

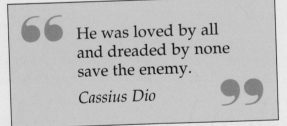

> He was loved by all and dreaded by none save the enemy.
>
> *Cassius Dio*

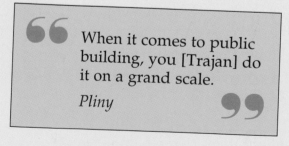

> When it comes to public building, you [Trajan] do it on a grand scale.
>
> *Pliny*

Bust of Trajan in the British Museum

The family says goodbye

Minimus strīdet et circum Iūlium currit.

valē, lūtī!

dea Fortūna! fīlium meum custōdī!

Lepidīna lacrimat.

 ## WORDS TO HELP

Nouns

cēnam (f) dinner
dōnum (n) present
fīlium (m) son
librum (m) book
vestīmenta (n plural) clothes

Pronoun

tibi for you

Idiom

grātiās tibi agō I thank you

Verbs

bibunt they drink
cape! take
colligit she collects
coquit he cooks
custōdī! take care of
habeō I have
mulcet he strokes
murmurat she purrs
pugnant they fight
rīdent they laugh
saltat she dances
strīdet he squeaks

Adjectives

frīgidus/a/um cold
meus/a/um my
parvus/a/um small

Adverbs

intentē closely
iocōsē playfully
lēniter gently
optimē very well
perītē skilfully
suāviter sweetly

> Nouns can be either **singular** (like "book") or **plural** (like "clothes").
> We'll mark plural nouns with a **pl** after the gender in "Words to help"
> from now on.

How do they feel?

Iulius is about to go on a long journey to Dacia and his family will not see him for a long time.

How do you think each of them feels about his journey? Imagine that Iulius was your older brother. How would you feel? Why will the journey be more dangerous for Iulius than it would be today?

GRASP THE GRAMMAR

In the picture story on pages 13 and 14 we saw that **adjectives** describe **nouns**, for example the emperor (**imperātor**) was described as "best" (**optimus**).

In this story, some of the **verbs** are made more interesting by adding an **adverb**. Adverbs tell us *how* the action is done, for example Pandora sings "sweetly". In English, many adverbs end in **-ly**.

But be careful! Some adverbs don't follow this pattern. For example, in the sentence "Vibrissa catches mice well", the word "well" is the adverb.

You can remember the word "adverb" because it **adds** to the **verb**.

Have another look at the picture story. See how many **adjectives** and **adverbs** you can find. Then make two columns, one for the adjectives and one for the adverbs. Write each word down in Latin first and then in English.

Corinthus tries to reassure Lepidina by telling the story of the famous Greek hero, Odysseus, who eventually arrived home safely after many exciting adventures.

ODYSSEUS AT SEA

After the Greeks defeated the Trojans and destroyed their city, they all set sail for Greece. The hero Odysseus took ten years to travel back to his home in Ithaca. This was because he had many adventures on the way. One day, he and his men had to sail past the Sirens. These were terrible creatures who had the heads and voices of women but the bodies of birds. They sang so sweetly that they lured passing sailors to their death on the rocks of their island. Odysseus

had a cunning plan. He was curious to hear the singing himself but he did not want to endanger his ship. He made his crew fill their ears with beeswax so that they could not hear the singing. Odysseus did not put wax in his own ears but asked his men to tie him securely to the mast of the ship. As they approached the Sirens and Odysseus heard their beautiful song, he was very tempted to leap overboard, but the ropes held him tightly and his men rowed frantically until they had sailed safely past.

A difficult journey

The family have finished packing their belongings. They set off on their journey in a covered wagon. Flavius rides in front and he has armed soldiers with him to protect his family.

WORDS TO HELP

Nouns

fossam (f) ditch
marītus (m) husband
plaustrum (n) wagon

Pronouns

mihi for me
tibi for you (singular)
nōbīs for us
vōbīs for you (plural)

Adverbs

iterum again
lentē slowly
tandem at last

Verbs

accipiunt they welcome
adiuvāte! help!
adveniunt they arrive
advesperāscit it is becoming dark
cavēte! be careful!
dēcidit it falls down
difficile est it is difficult
intrāte! come in!
necesse est it is necessary
pluit it is raining
sedet it sits
tonat it thunders

Infinitives

cantāre to sing
dēscendere to climb down
prōpellere to push

Adjectives

exspectātissimus/a/um
  very welcome
līmōsus/a/um muddy
lūbricus/a/um slippery
perterritus/a/um frightened
tacitus/a/um silent

Preposition

ē from

GRASP THE GRAMMAR

Remember that a **verb** is an action word!

In this story you have met some new **verb endings**.

Look at **cantāre**. It means "to sing". We call this form of the verb the **infinitive**. Have another look at pictures 5 and 6. Try to find two more infinitives. What does each one mean?

Remember, the infinitive usually ends in **-re** and the translation begins "to . . ." (to run, to eat, etc.).

We also met some verbs like **pluit** which means "it is raining". When the subject of a verb is "it" we call it an **impersonal verb**. Look at pictures 1, 5, 6, 8 and 9. Try to find six uses of impersonal verbs.

Now translate the following sentences. When you have translated them, write down in Latin all the **impersonal verbs** and all the **infinitives** that you can find. Again, some have been used more than once.

Be careful! Some have been used more than once.

Here is a clue to help you: I can find 13 impersonal verbs . . .

. . . and I can find eight infinitives.

1 in Britanniā semper pluit.
2 Vibrissa dīcit, "iterum pluit. necesse est mihi currere."
3 Vibrissa dīcit, "difficile est mihi currere quod obēsa sum."
4 Lepidīna dīcit, "Rūfe, advesperāscit. necesse est tibi dormīre."
5 Rūfus dīcit, "sed difficile est mihi dormīre quod fessus nōn sum."
6 Lepidīna dīcit, "advesperāscit. necesse est nōbīs festīnāre."
7 Flāvius dīcit, "sed difficile est nōbīs festīnāre quod via lūbrica est."
8 Rūfus dīcit, "iterum tonat. perterritus sum."
9 Pandōra dīcit, "Rūfe, nōlī timēre! necesse est mihi cantāre."
10 Rūfus dīcit, "nunc nōn tonat. euge!"

If you pronounce **necesse** and **difficile** properly, you will always spell the words "necessary" and "difficult" correctly in English!

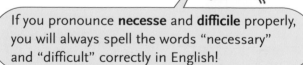

How do they feel?

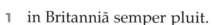

The family set off on their journey. They sit in silence. Try to imagine what each of them feels as they move to their new home in Eboracum. Describe the feelings of each person (Flavius, Lepidina, Rufus, Vibrissa, Minimus, Corinthus, Candidus and Pandora).

LATIN ROOTS

Use your knowledge of Latin to explain the underlined word in each sentence.

1 There is something wrong with my car engine. I think it needs some <u>lubricating</u> oil.

2 The boat could not move because the <u>propeller</u> was stuck in the mud.

3 Pavarotti will be performing a famous <u>cantata</u> in Verona.

4 I need to change my <u>sedentary</u> job and get more exercise.

Do you play a musical instrument? Usually the instructions on how to play a piece are given in Italian, a language which has developed from Latin.
So how would you play if the music said **lente**?

ROMAN REPORT

Roman roads

The Romans were famous for building straight roads wherever they went. They built their roads as straight as possible so that soldiers could march quickly and avoid the risk of ambush. The roads linked Rome with the various countries that they conquered. In Britain, the Romans built approximately 13,000 kilometres (8,000 miles) of roads. Parts of them survive today and in many places we can still walk or drive along the line of a Roman road.

Most of the road building was done by legionary soldiers. They dug a ditch on either side of the road to drain away any rainwater. Then they used the earth and rubble that they had dug out to build up the ground between the ditches into a mound. On top of this, they put large stones and then a layer of small stones. Finally, they used large, shaped stones as a top layer, fitted together tightly. This is known as "metalling". The surface of the road was normally slightly curved, to allow rainwater to drain off. Roman roads were up to eight metres wide.

If the road was good, soldiers could march up to 30 miles a day. People also rode on mules or donkeys. In one of the Vindolanda writing tablets, a centurion complains that supplies to Catterick have been held up because the road there is a bad one.

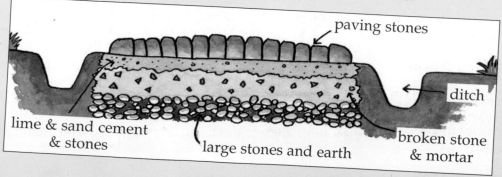

paving stones

ditch

lime & sand cement & stones

large stones and earth

broken stone & mortar

Flavia is not well

Flavia's slave has prepared a special welcome dinner for the family.

Panel 7: euge! servī! plūs vīnī! necesse est mihi propīnāre. grātulātiōnēs!

Panel 8: ubi est obstetrīx bona? necesse est tibi quiēscere.

Lepidīna Flāviam īnspicit.

Panel 9: ego avus erō! ego avia erō!

Lepidīna et Flāvius laetī sunt.

Panel 10: deae mātrēs! fīliam meam custōdīte!

sed Lepidīna anxia est.

 WORDS TO HELP

Nouns

avia (f) grandmother
avus (m) grandfather
cibus (m) food
deae mātrēs (f pl) mother goddesses
obstetrīx (f) midwife
pāvō (m) peacock
triclīnium (n) dining room

Verbs

adest it is here
cōnsūmunt they eat
erō I will be
īnspicit s/he inspects
revenit she returns
sedē! sit down!

Infinitives
propīnāre to propose a toast
quiēscere to rest

Adjectives

gravidus/a/um pregnant; heavy
modicus/a/um ordinary

Adverbs

celeriter quickly
cotīdiē every day
minimē! no!

Idioms

plūs vīnī more wine
quid agis? what's the matter?
vir optime! sir!

Exclamation

grātulātiōnēs! (f pl) congratulations!

Lepidina is still feeling rather worried about her daughter.
Corinthus tries to distract her by telling a Greek story.
Soon Lepidina is smiling.

A VERY STRANGE BIRTH

Once upon a time Zeus, the king of the gods, fell in love with a sea goddess called Metis. Mother Earth warned Zeus that any child born of this friendship with Metis would overthrow him. Zeus was taking no chances. When he got near to Metis, he swallowed her whole. Almost immediately he began to have violent headaches: it felt as if his head would burst. He howled so loudly that he shook Mount Olympus. Hermes realised what was wrong and went to fetch Hephaestus, the blacksmith god. Hephaestus split open Zeus's skull with an axe. Out sprang Athene, the warrior goddess, fully armed and uttering battle cries. What an unusual birth! Of course, because he was king of the gods, Zeus soon recovered.

After saying goodbye to Flavia and Gaius, the family eventually arrives in Eboracum. Their new home is near the soldiers' fortress. They set off to explore . . .

Discovering Eboracum

WORDS TO HELP

Nouns

amīcus (m) friend
amphorīs (f pl) jars
clāvī (m pl) nails
ferrārius (m) blacksmith
figlīnā (f) pottery workshop
figulus (m) potter
flūmen (n) river
fornāx (f) forge
frūmentum (n) grain
horreum (n) granary
nāvēs (f pl) ships
ōllae (f pl) pots
paterae (f pl) bowls
vexillārius (m) flag-seller

Verb

Infinitive
condere to store

Pronoun
tū you (sing.)

Preposition
cum with

GRASP THE GRAMMAR

When we're telling a story, we don't want to keep repeating the names of all the main characters. For example, "Barates comes from Syria. Barates is a flag-seller. Barates shows the family around Eboracum."

In place of the name Barates, it's much easier to use the word "he". Words that stand in the place of nouns are called **pronouns**.

In English we use pronouns much more often than in Latin. Remember that in chapter 1 you learnt that Latin verbs don't need a separate word to show *who* is doing the action. The **verb ending** tells us who is doing it. So if we want to say "he shows" in Latin, we can just say **dēmōnstrat**. If we want to say "I show", we just say **dēmōnstrō**.

The Romans only used pronouns for emphasis or to make a contrast, for example "*I* support Newcastle but *you* are a Liverpool fan."

Look back at pictures 3 and 5 on page 27. Find the two little Latin words that mean "I" and "you". These are called **personal pronouns**. Remember that they are only used for emphasis.

Redraft this paragraph, replacing the nouns with pronouns.

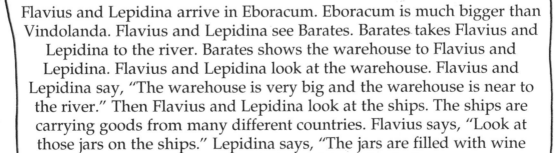

Flavius and Lepidina arrive in Eboracum. Eboracum is much bigger than Vindolanda. Flavius and Lepidina see Barates. Barates takes Flavius and Lepidina to the river. Barates shows the warehouse to Flavius and Lepidina. Flavius and Lepidina look at the warehouse. Flavius and Lepidina say, "The warehouse is very big and the warehouse is near to the river." Then Flavius and Lepidina look at the ships. The ships are carrying goods from many different countries. Flavius says, "Look at those jars on the ships." Lepidina says, "The jars are filled with wine from France and olive oil from Spain."

LATIN ROOTS

Use your knowledge of Latin to work out the meaning of the underlined word in each sentence.

1. We parked in the <u>multi-storey</u> car park.
2. If we go to the <u>multiplex</u> cinema we can choose which film we want to watch.
3. Now that I am studying Latin, French and Italian I am becoming <u>multi-lingual</u>.
4. Most of our big cities are <u>multi-racial</u>.
5. To make 100, we <u>multiply</u> 25 by 4.
6. Why did the film producer call the famous gladiator "<u>Maximus</u>"?

ROMAN REPORT

Eboracum (York)

About one hundred years after Flavius and his family came to live there, Eboracum became one of the most important Roman towns in Britain. It began as a wooden fortress for soldiers towards the end of the first century AD. Then a small settlement grew up outside the fortress; this provided accommodation for the merchants, traders and families who followed the troops. This is how many Roman towns began.

Flavius and the family are seeing Eboracum in the very early stages of its development. The buildings outside the fortress are made of wood, or wattle and daub. There are craftsmen selling their products and many more goods come up the River Ouse from various parts of the Roman Empire. On the far side of the river there is a series of warehouses. Each one stores different items, for example there is one for wool and one for grain (a granary).

Flavius and his family have a big house near the military fortress. There are plans to build a new fortress out of stone. Flavius's new job is to supervise the planning and design of this new military headquarters. When the local people realise that the old wooden fortress is going to be replaced by a stone one, they know that the Roman army is here to stay.

The granary is destroyed

The next day, Rufus notices that workmen are pulling down the granary.

 WORDS TO HELP

Nouns

digitōs (m pl) fingers
fabrī (m pl) workmen
ligna (n pl) wooden planks
scarabaeī (m pl) beetles

Adjectives

cārus/a/um expensive
foedus/a/um disgusting
iūcundus/a/um lovely
malus/a/um bad
mīlia thousands

Verbs

dēlent they destroy
dētrahunt they remove
labōrant they work
nōlī tangere! don't touch!
sistite! stop!
venī! come!

Infinitives
lavāre to wash
tollere to remove

Impersonal verb
facile est nōbīs it is easy for us

Idiom

mēcum with me

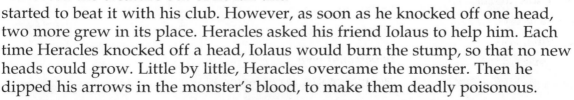

ROMAN REPORT

Archaeologists working in Eboracum have found out a great deal about the granary. When they examined the remains of the grain carefully under a microscope, they could clearly see dead beetles in it. It seems that this grain was so badly infested that the soldiers in the fortress decided it would be best to pull down the granary and start again. They put down a layer of clay and then started to build the new granary. It too was made of wood and, unfortunately, it appears that it burnt down. Archaeologists have found the remains of a lot of burnt grain in Eboracum. Timber buildings were always at risk but stone granaries were not built until later.

This microscope slide shows
a grain beetle and charred grain

Pulling down the warehouse to get rid of the beetles is a long and difficult task. It reminds Corinthus of a famous Greek hero, who also had to destroy a terrible scourge.

HERACLES AND THE HYDRA

In Greece, at a place called Lerna, there lived a fearsome water-snake. It was called the Hydra and it was a terrible watery monster with many snaky necks and fanged, poison-dripping heads. It lived in a dismal swamp, feeding off the crops and flocks, and its venomous breath spread death.

Heracles was set twelve very difficult tasks. One of these was to kill the Hydra. He forced the creature out of its lair and started to beat it with his club. However, as soon as he knocked off one head, two more grew in its place. Heracles asked his friend Iolaus to help him. Each time Heracles knocked off a head, Iolaus would burn the stump, so that no new heads could grow. Little by little, Heracles overcame the monster. Then he dipped his arrows in the monster's blood, to make them deadly poisonous.

Sad news

Flavius has been visiting the soldiers in the fortress and has heard some sad news.

1. cārissime, cūr tam trīstis es?
   quod Duccius mortuus est.
2. quis Duccius est?
   Lūcius Duccius Rūfīnus mīles optimus erat. signifer erat.
3. quid signifer est?
   signifer signum in proelium portat.
4. signifer quoque stīpendium cūrat. signifer stīpendium sub sacellō custōdit.
5. mihi placet sculptōrem optimum invenīre.
   Flāvius celeriter exit.
6. salvē!
   salvē! quid vīs?
   Flāvius officīnam intrat.

WORDS TO HELP

Nouns

diēs (m pl) days

iuvenis (m) young man

phalerae (f pl) medals

proelium (n) battle

sacellum (n) chapel

signifer (m) standard-bearer

signum (n) military standard

stīpendium (n) pay (for soldiers)

titulus (m) inscription

Verbs

cūrat he looks after

custōdit he guards

erat he was

volō I want

vīs you want

Infinitives

facere to make

invenīre to find

sculpere to carve

Impersonal verbs

mihi placet I want (it pleases me)

tibi licet you are allowed / you may (it is permitted for you)

Adjectives

cārissime dearest

paucōs a few

trīstis sad

Prepositions

post after

sub under

Adverb

tam so

GRASP THE GRAMMAR

In the picture story, there are two new **impersonal verbs**:
(mihi) placet and **(tibi) licet**.

The literal translation of these two verbs is "it is pleasing (to me)"
and "it is permitted (for you)".

But people don't talk like that! Our translation into English needs to sound
natural as well as being accurate. So it's much better to translate these verbs
as "I want" and "you can" or "you are allowed".

Did you remember the question words? What's
the difference between **cūr?**, **quis?** and **quid?**

Have another look at the picture story. Can
you find the five **infinitives**? Remember that
they all end in **-re**. One of them is used twice.

 LATIN ROOTS

Use your knowledge of Latin to explain the underlined words.

1 At the trial, the judge ordered the defendant to be remanded
  in <u>custody</u>.

2 At our school, games are <u>voluntary</u> for sixth-formers.

3 James Bond – <u>licensed</u> to kill.

4 Most teachers cannot tolerate <u>juvenile</u> behaviour.

5 As the old lady died in suspicious circumstances,
  there will be a <u>post-mortem</u> in the <u>mortuary</u>.

6 Was the printing press a more significant <u>invention</u>
  than television?

ROMAN REPORT

The signifer (standard-bearer)

Each unit of the Roman army had its own military "standard" – a sign or emblem identifying its part of the legion. It was carried by the standard-bearer (**signifer**), one of the officers in the Roman army. He carried the standard with pride and it was a source of great shame and dishonour if the standard was lost to the enemy. The carvings on Trajan's column show that the standard-bearer usually wore scale armour (made in overlapping sections) and a bearskin, and carried a small, round shield.

The standard-bearer was also in charge of the soldiers' pay. This money was kept in a locked room beneath the **sacellum** or chapel of the military fortress.

The tombstone of Lucius Duccius Rufinus, now in the Yorkshire Museum

Here is Lucius Duccius, the standard-bearer. In his right hand he is holding the military standard. Can you see the **phalerae** on the pole, with a hand at the top? In his left hand, Lucius is holding a set of writing tablets. What do you think is written on these tablets?

Notice that Lucius is not wearing a bearskin but an unusual Celtic woollen cloak, called a **paenula**. The inscription beneath the figure tells us more about Lucius.

You need to look at some of the abbreviations:

1 LEG. is short for **legiō**. The Roman numerals tell us his legion. Which legion did Lucius belong to?

2 AN. is short for **annōs**, which means "years". Can you find out how old Lucius was when he died?

3 VIEN. is short for **Vienne**. This tells us that Lucius was from Vienne in Gaul (now France) rather than from Austria.

Why do you think Flavius had this tombstone made for Lucius Duccius?

A letter from Dacia

1 Lepidīna laeta est.
Lepidīna epistulam tenet.
Lepidīna epistulam legit.

2 Dācia frīgida est. saepe pluit.

3 nunc ningit!

4 aliī mīlitēs pontem aedificant.

5 pōns trāns Dānuvium trānsit.
pōns mīrus est. sunt multa saxa.

6 necesse est mīlitibus dīligenter labōrāre et saxa portāre.

7. aliī mīlitēs fortiter pugnant. ego tamen nōn pugnō quod scrība sum.

8. Trāiānus dux optimus est. Trāiānus cum mīlitibus edit.

9. euge! Iūlius tūtus est!

Flāvius et Rūfus et servī laetī sunt.

10. sed Lepidīna anxia est, quod māter est.

Dācia frīgida est. bellum perīculōsum est . . .

 WORDS TO HELP

Nouns

Dānuvius (m) the River Danube
dux (m) leader
epistula (f) letter
pōns (m) bridge
saxum (n) stone
scrība (m) secretary

Verbs

legit she reads
pugnō I fight
pugnant they fight
tenet she holds
trānsit it crosses

Infinitives
labōrāre to work
portāre to carry

Impersonal verb
ningit it is snowing

Adverb

tamen however

Adjective

tūtus/a/um safe

Rufus is curious about the weather in Dacia. Corinthus tells him the story of the seasons.

DEMETER AND PERSEPHONE

Demeter, the goddess of crops and of all growing things, bore Zeus a beautiful daughter called Persephone. One day Persephone was out gathering poppies when she was spied by Hades, the god of the Underworld. Hades decided to carry her off to the Underworld to live with him. As he abducted her, she shrieked so loudly that her cries reached her mother. Demeter mourned the loss of her daughter and so did the whole of nature. Flowers wilted, the fields lay bare and fruit rotted on the branches.

Zeus was alarmed so he sent Hermes to Hades, asking him to release Persephone. Hades agreed to let her go but only on condition that she had not eaten anything. As Persephone had already eaten six pomegranate seeds, she could only return to earth for six months of the year.

She returned to her mother and immediately all the flowers began to bloom and the crops to grow. This was the beginning of spring and summer. But when Persephone returned to the Underworld, all the crops stopped growing and the leaves fluttered down from the trees. It grew cold and dark – autumn and winter had begun. From then on, Persephone spent six lovely months on earth and six dark months in the Underworld and that is why we have the changing seasons.

It's the Saturnalia!

1. Sāturnālia adsunt.
Flāvia et Gāius vīsitant.

2. Lepidīna cēnam coquit.

3. *cibus optimus est!*
Candidus cibum gustat.

4. Pandōra in lectō recumbit.
Pandōra pilleum gerit.

5. Corinthus et Candidus quoque recumbunt.
Corinthus et Candidus pilleōs gerunt.

6. *hodiē servī sumus!*
Flāvius et Rūfus cibum portant.

WORDS TO HELP

Nouns

cibus (m) food

lectus (m) couch

pilleus (m) cap of freedom

Sāturnālia (n pl) Saturnalia
 (festival in December)

Preposition

in in/on

Verbs

adsunt (they) are here

dētergit he cleans up

fundit he pours

gerit she wears

gustat he tastes

lacrimat he cries

profundit he spills

recumbit she reclines

Adjectives

benignus/a/um kind

pulcher/pulchra/pulchrum
 beautiful

Adverb

hodiē today

GRASP THE GRAMMAR

> It's time to practise some **verbs**.

Remember to look at the **ending** of a verb to see who is doing the action.

What do the following verbs mean in English? Remember to say if it is "he" or "they" doing the action.

> Look back at the picture story if you are stuck with any of the meanings.

1 lacrimat	4 recumbunt	7 vīsitat
2 vīsitant	5 portant	8 fundit
3 recumbit	6 lacrimant	9 portat

> **Nouns** change their endings too, to show what job they are doing in the sentence.

Compare these two sentences:

a **Pandōra** pilleum gerit.   Pandora is wearing a cap.

b Candidus **Pandōram** spectat.   Candidus looks at Pandora.

In sentence **a**, Pandora is the person doing the action. We say that she is the **subject** of the sentence.

In sentence **b**, she has the action done to her. Pandora is the **object** of this sentence and so the ending of the noun **Pandōra** now becomes **Pandōram**.

ROMAN REPORT

The Saturnalia

The Saturnalia was the most important holiday in the Roman year. The Latin poet Catullus describes it as "**optimus diērum**", the best of days. It began on 17 December and lasted for up to seven days. The festival was named after the god Saturnus, whom the Romans thought of as a god of liberation. Saturnalia was therefore a time of freedom, when a slave and his master exchanged their roles; the slave wore a **pilleus**, a cap of freedom. This was the cap that slaves wore if they were granted their freedom in a formal ceremony. It was also a time for wearing the **synthesis**, a long, loose, unbelted tunic.

The Saturnalia involved feasting, music and dancing, sacrifices and shows. People also told jokes and gave each other presents. These might be toys, books, jewellery or cosmetics. Candles and small statuettes made from terracotta, called **sigillāria**, were also popular presents.

Which of these Roman customs do we still follow when we celebrate Christmas?

Time for presents!

1 post cēnam Lepidīna perītē saltat.

2 omnēs servī hilariter cantant.

3 tōta familia iocōs facit.

4 necesse est mihi dōna invenīre.

Lepidīna exit.

5 Lepidīna in triclīnium revenit.

Rūfe! hoc dōnum tuum est!

Rūfus pilam accipit.

6 Corinthe! hoc dōnum tuum est!

Corinthus librum accipit.

7 Candide! hoc dōnum tuum est!

Candidus candēlam accipit.

8 cārissime! hoc dōnum tuum est!

Flāvius ānulum accipit.

9 Lepidīna! hoc dōnum tuum est!

Lepidīna quoque ānulum accipit.

10 ubi dōna nostra sunt?

ecce!

WORDS TO HELP

Nouns

ānulus (m) ring
dōna (n pl) presents
iocōs (m pl) jokes
pila (f) ball

Verbs

accipit he receives

Infinitive
invenīre to find

Adjectives

noster/nostra/nostrum our
tuus/tua/tuum your

Adverb

hilariter cheerfully

GRASP THE GRAMMAR

In picture 4, Lepidina says that she has to find the presents. In Latin, this is expressed by an **impersonal verb** plus an **infinitive**:

I must

necesse est mihi dōna invenīre.   It is necessary for me to find the presents.

Using two other **impersonal verbs**, write down in Latin:

a It is difficult for me to find the presents.

b It is easy for me to find the presents.

 LATIN ROOTS

From the picture stories in this chapter, find the meaning of the underlined word in each sentence.

1. The surgeon was pleased to see that the growth was <u>benign</u>; the man's life was not in danger.
2. I'm collecting for charity and am hoping for plenty of <u>donations</u>.
3. The stain is so bad that it will need a strong <u>detergent</u> to remove it.
4. Now that my sister has had her baby, she must take him to the <u>post-natal</u> clinic.

MUDDLED PRESENTS

The family have some other Saturnalia presents for one another but they are in a muddle. Can you sort them out and find a suitable present for each person?

Flāvius
ampulla
perfume bottle

Gāius
pila
ball

Flāvia
ūdōnēs
socks

Rūfus
capillāmentum
wig

Pandōra
scōpae
broom

Candidus
scrīnium
bookcase

Corinthus
sāpō
hair dye

Lepidīna
vēnābula
hunting spears

What Saturnalia presents do you think Minimus and Vibrissa might give each other?

Try to find out the Latin word for the presents that you choose.

These are like the rings which Flavius and Lepidina exchanged. Flavius's ring has an intaglio of Mars; Lepidina's has an intaglio of Fortuna. Why do you think these are particularly suitable presents?

Intaglios from Roman rings found in a sewer in York

The whole family is tired and happy after the Saturnalia. Rufus asks Corinthus how the festival came to be called the Saturnalia. Corinthus explains . . .

SATURN AND THE GOLDEN AGE

Jupiter banished his father, Saturn, from Mount Olympus and became king of the gods in his place. Saturn wandered the earth until eventually he came to Italy, where he became king of Latium. He taught his subjects the skills of agriculture and the blessings of civilisation. People thought of his rule as a Golden Age. Everyone lived peacefully together and life was prosperous. Since those happy times, people have celebrated Saturn's festival, the Saturnalia, with feasting, freedom and happiness – they try to re-create his Golden Age for a few days.

Lepidina decides to return to Cataractonium to help Flavia when the baby arrives. She is closely followed by the rest of the family.

The great day arrives

1 necesse est mihi Flāviam adiuvāre.

Lepidīna ad Cataractōnium revenit.

2 nunc īnfāns advenit! adiuvā! māter, adiuvā!

Flāvia maximē dolet.

3 nōlī timēre! necesse est mihi obstetrīcem arcessere.

ita vērō. celeriter!

4 nōlite timēre! Flāvia, valida es. Lepidīna, aquam portā!

obstetrīx advenit.

5 Lepidīna aquam et sūdāria portat. tum obstetrīx et Lepidīna digitōs lavant.

6 Flāvia! nōlī anxia esse! relaxā!

obstetrīx Flāviam adiuvat.

 WORDS TO HELP

Nouns

aqua (f) water
fīlia (f) daughter
geminī (m pl) twins
īnfāns (m *or* f) baby
sūdārium (n) towel

Verbs

adiuvā! help!
advenit he/she arrives
dolet she is in pain
lavant they wash
manē! wait!

Infinitives
adiuvāre to help
arcessere to call for
timēre to be afraid

Adjectives

alter/altera/alterum another
validus/a/um strong

Adverbs

hūc illūc here
  and there/up and down
intereā meanwhile

GRASP THE GRAMMAR

> That midwife was giving a lot of orders!

Latin uses a particular form of the verb for giving orders: it is called an **imperative**.

Look back at pictures 2, 4, 6 and 9. What do these orders mean?

adiuvā! portā! relaxā! manē!

Now look at pictures 1 and 2 again. There are two very similar words here – **adiuvāre** and **adiuvā!**

The first form (**adiuvāre**) is the **infinitive** and it means "to help".

The second form is like the infinitive, but without the final **-re**. **adiuvā!** is the **imperative** or **command** form and it means "help!"

> Sometimes we want to tell someone **not** to do something.

In Latin we use the words **nōlī** or **nōlīte**, which mean "don't". These words are followed by the **infinitive**.

> Look at pictures 3 and 4. Find the two Latin phrases that mean "Don't be afraid!"

> Why do you think the first one uses **nōlī** but the second uses **nōlīte**?

Here are some more **imperatives** for you to practise. Be careful – some are **negative** and some are **positive**, and some are **singular** and some are **plural**. Translate the phrases and say whether each one is **singular** or **plural**.

1 digitōs lavāte!
2 nōlīte dormīre!
3 nōlī lacrimāre!
4 aquam portāte!
5 nōlī currere!

6 festīnāte!
7 cantāte!
8 nōlīte pugnāre!
9 aedificā!
10 intrāte!

LATIN ROOTS

Use your knowledge of Latin to work out the meaning of the underlined words.

1 Roman engineers built lots of famous <u>aqueducts</u>.
2 If you learn your vocabulary thoroughly you should gain <u>maximum</u> points in the test.
3 The dog ate your homework? That is not a <u>valid</u> excuse.
4 In Roman times, many <u>invalids</u> came to Bath to take the waters, hoping for a cure.
5 When I study medicine, part of my course will be <u>obstetrics</u>.

Everyone welcomes the twins

1 Gāius cubiculum intrat.
Gāius geminōs in terram pōnit.

2 geminī validī sunt.
Larēs geminōs accipiunt.

subitō geminī vāgiunt. omnēs laetī sunt.

3 obstetrīx geminōs lavat et involvit.

4 quam pulchrī sunt!

Gāius geminōs tenet.

5 tū avus es! et tū avia es!

et ego avunculus sum!

Flāvius et Rūfus intrant.

6 necesse est nōbīs astrologum arcessere.

Gāius exit.

7 astrologus stēllās īnspicit et intrat.

8 geminī sub caprā nātī sunt. horoscopus bonus est!

9 hic puer fortis et validus erit.

astrologus fīlium tenet.

10 haec puella valida et honesta erit.

astrologus fīliam tenet.

WORDS TO HELP

Nouns	Verbs	Adjectives
avunculus (m) uncle	**erit** he/she will be	**fortis/fortis/forte** brave
capra (f) she-goat	**involvit** she wraps up	**honestus/a/um**
cubiculum (n) bedroom	**pōnit** he puts	honourable/virtuous
Larēs (m pl) the	**tenet** he holds	
household gods	**vāgiunt** they wail	**Pronouns**
stēllās (f pl) stars		**hic/haec** this
terra (f) ground		

ROMAN REPORT

Having a baby

We can find evidence about Roman childbirth customs in the works of the ancient writer Soranus. The Romans were uncertain about the normal length of pregnancy, so Flavia would not have been sure when her baby was due. Without the benefit of an ultrasound scanner, no one could have known that she was expecting twins.

The normal practice was for Roman babies to be born at home, with the help of a midwife. A doctor was only called if there were complications. In Germany, as soon as a baby was born, it would be put onto the ground; this was to introduce it to the household gods. If the baby cried loudly, this was a sign of its acceptance by the gods. If the baby's father then picked up the child, this was a sign that it was worth rearing. Only then would the baby be washed and wrapped up warmly.

The Romans were eager to know the future, especially when a baby was born. They would consult an astrologer, who would read the baby's horoscope. The baby would then be named at a special ceremony.

Wet nurses or foster parents, and symbol of local god of Petrovio, relief, 2nd–3rd century AD Roman

THE SOUND OF LATIN

In the picture story we met the word **vāgiunt** (they wail). This is an appropriate word, as the sound of the word resembles its meaning. Words like this are called **onomatopoeic** words. English examples include "crash", "bang" and "cuckoo". You have already met two other Latin examples of onomatopoeia – **euge!** and **ēheu!** Other examples include **susurrāre** (to whisper), **ululāre** (to howl) and **pīpiāre** (to chirp). Look out for more examples in your reading of both Latin and English.

Rufus is very interested in the twins. Flavius tells him the story
of the most famous twins in Roman history.

ROMULUS AND REMUS

Long, long ago in Italy, King Numitor of Alba Longa was forced into exile by
his jealous brother, Amulius. Amulius seized the throne. He realised he had to
prevent Numitor's heirs from threatening his position. He murdered Numitor's
sons and tried to prevent Rhea Silvia, Numitor's lovely daughter, from having
children of her own. His evil scheme was foiled when the god Mars fell in love
with Rhea Silvia and she gave birth to twin sons. Furious, Amulius imprisoned
her and ordered the babies to be thrown into the River Tiber. But the twins
survived: they were in a basket that floated ashore. A she-wolf suckled the baby

boys and a woodpecker fed them scraps.
Eventually a shepherd, called Faustinus,
heard their cries. He took the boys home
and he and his wife brought them up.

One day, the brothers were captured and
handed over to Numitor. He suspected
that these boys were his grandsons.
Together they attacked and killed
Amulius, and Numitor became king
once more. Eventually, the twins set
off to found a city of their own but
they quarrelled and Remus was killed.
So Romulus was left to found a new
city alone; he called it Rome.

Romulus, Remus and the
she-wolf from a mosaic found in
Aldborough in Yorkshire

Rufus's first Greek lesson

Flavius has decided that it is time for Rufus to learn Greek.
Corinthus has found an expert teacher who lives in Eboracum.

 WORDS TO HELP

Nouns

Calēdonia (f) Scotland
deīs (m pl) to the gods
grammaticus (m) teacher
litterae (f pl) letters
nautae (m pl) sailors
nāvis (f) ship
portus (m) harbour
tabulae (f pl) tablets
tempestās (f) storm

Verbs

efflābat it was blowing
erat it was
habitās you live
iactābat it was tossing
nāvigābam I was sailing
ōrābam I was praying
pluēbat it was raining
timēbās you were frightened
volēbam I was wanting/I wanted

Infinitives
dōnāre to give/to donate
grātiās agere to thank
legere to read

Adjectives

novus/a/um new
turbulentus/a/um stormy
ventōsus/a/um windy

Adverbs

nūper recently
tandem at last

GRASP THE GRAMMAR

In the picture story, Demetrius is telling the story of his voyage around the Western Isles of Scotland. His journey has now finished, so he describes it to Rufus using a **past tense**.

> Verbs describe actions that happen in the past, the present or the future.

The new tense in the story is a past tense called the **imperfect tense**.

This is what it looks like in full:

nāvigā**bam**	I was sailing
nāvigā**bās**	you (*sing*) were sailing
nāvigā**bat**	he/she/it was sailing
nāvigā**bāmus**	we were sailing
nāvigā**bātis**	you (*pl*) were sailing
nāvigā**bant**	they were sailing

Have another look at pictures 3, 4, 5, 6, 7 and 9. Try to find ten examples of the **imperfect tense**. Write them down and translate them. Make sure you check the **ending** of the verb to see who is doing the action.

> Again, the verb "to be" is an exception. In picture 5, the imperfect tense of "to be" is used twice. The word is **erat** which means "he/she/it was".

 LATIN ROOTS

Use your knowledge of Latin to explain the underlined word in each sentence.

1 <u>Navigation</u> was extremely dangerous in the ancient world.
2 *The Rime of the Ancient <u>Mariner</u>* is a long poem by Coleridge.
3 My friend had a successful career as a <u>naval</u> captain.
4 Some people disapprove of zoos; they believe that animals should live in their natural <u>habitat</u>.
5 The pilot advised us to fasten our seat belts as we were experiencing some <u>turbulence</u>.
6 Shakespeare named one of his plays *The <u>Tempest</u>* because of the events in the first scene.

ROMAN REPORT

Roman seafaring

For the Romans, sailing was extremely hazardous. Maps of the world were rare and inaccurate and, with no compasses or modern navigational equipment, sailors had to find their way by the stars. Roman sailors preferred not to venture into the open sea. Instead they sailed short distances from port to port, following the coastline and using familiar landmarks. During the winter months they did not sail at all. At the beginning of spring, sailors celebrated the fact that they could now set out to sea again. It was quite normal to pray to the gods for safety or even make a sacrifice at the beginning of a voyage.

The teacher in the story, Scribonius Demetrius, was so thankful for his safe voyage around Scotland that he dedicated two bronze tablets to the sea gods, Oceanus and Tethys. These tablets are written in Greek and they are now in the Yorkshire Museum.

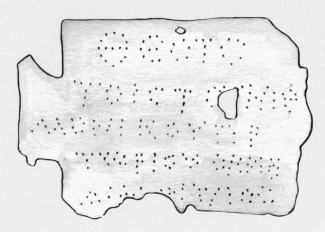

To the gods of the governor's residence. Scrib(onius) Demetrius.

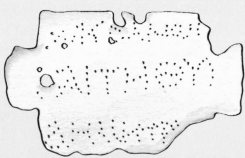

To Ocean and Tethys. Demetrius.

The Greek is written in dots punched into the metal and the writing is all in capitals. It is not easy to read!

Rufus learns his letters

 WORDS TO HELP

Nouns

annōs (m pl) years
frondēs (f pl) leaves, herbs
ōrāculum (n) oracle
Pȳthia (f) the Pythia (name of priestess at Delphi)
respōnsa Apollonis Apollo's answers
sacerdōs (f) priestess
tripode (m) tripod

Verbs

cōnsulēbam I was consulting
discit he learns
mandēbat she was chewing
prōferēbat she was uttering
sedēbat she was sitting

Infinitive
scrībere to write

Impersonal verb
necesse erit tibi you will have to

Pronoun

hās these

Adverbs

diū for a long time
praecipuē especially

Preposition

ante before/ago

Adjective

clārus/a/um famous

GRASP THE GRAMMAR

> Remember that the most important word in a sentence is the **verb** or action word.

You've now met verbs in several different forms.

> Let's have a look at the verb **scrībere** which means "to write".

Here are the different endings that you have met:

- scrī**bere** (to write) This is called the **infinitive**.
- scrī**bō** (I write/I am writing) This is the **present tense**. The rest of the present tense looks like this:

  scrī**bis**, scrī**bit**, scrī**bimus**, scrī**bitis**, scrī**bunt**.

- scrī**bēbam** (I was writing) This is the **imperfect tense**, the new tense that you have met in this chapter. The rest of the imperfect tense looks like this:

  scrī**bēbās**, scrī**bēbat**, scrī**bēbāmus**, scrī**bēbātis**, scrī**bēbant**.

- scrī**be**! scrī**bite**! (write!) This is called the **imperative**, or **command** or **order**.
- Then there are **impersonal verbs**, such as **necesse est**, which have "it" as the subject (it is necessary).

> Now let's see if you can recognise all these different verb forms.

Look back at the picture story. In each picture, pick out the Latin **verbs**. Say whether each one is an **infinitive**, or the **present** or **imperfect tense**, or whether it is an **impersonal verb**.

> Watch out! There are no commands in this story but some sentences have more than one verb.

ROMAN REPORT

Delphi

Delphi was an important place for the ancient Greeks and Romans. According to legend, Zeus sent out two eagles to locate the centre of the earth. Their paths crossed at Delphi and a great stone called the **omphalos** (or 'navel stone') was erected to mark the spot. The whole sanctuary of Delphi was dedicated to Apollo, the god of prophecy. For over 1,000 years, people came here to consult the oracle when they needed to solve a dilemma. After sacrificing an animal, they would go to consult the Pythian priestess. After the

priestess had purified herself, she sat on the sacred tripod, went into a trance and gave a response from the god himself. Her replies were often ambiguous. For example, King Croesus of Lydia asked if he should go to war against the Persians. The priestess replied, "If you do, you will destroy a great empire." Croesus went to war and he did indeed destroy a mighty empire – his own.

The ancient site of Delphi

Rufus has had a busy day, learning the Greek alphabet and finding out all about the world of the Greeks. Corinthus comes in and, together, he and Demetrius tell Rufus about the gods of the ocean.

OCEANUS AND TETHYS

Oceanus was the eldest of the Titans; he was both a god and a river. He surrounded the whole of the earth. Every day, the sun and the stars rose and set in the ocean. Oceanus married his sister, Tethys, who was goddess of the sea-creatures. Fishes were known as Tethys's cattle. Oceanus and Tethys had three thousand sons and three thousand daughters and one foster-daughter, Hera, the queen of the gods. Hera's husband, Zeus, often hurt and angered her with his infidelities. When he fell in love with a nymph called Callisto and proposed to set her image among the stars as a constellation, Hera fled to her foster-parents for support. Tethys refused to let Callisto's constellation, the Great Bear, touch the waters of the ocean at the end of the night. This is why the Great Bear is the only constellation that never sets below the horizon.

The twins are named

Back at home in Eboracum, Lepidina and Rufus are describing to Pandora the two special days when the twins were named.

1. octāvō diē amīcī et cognātī ad vīllam veniēbant.

2. diēs lūstricus erat. Gāius fīliam tenēbat.

3. nōmen tuum Gāia Charisa est.
Gāius aquam in fīliam spargēbat.

4. omnēs dōna dabant. omnēs laetissimī erant.

5. Rūfus animālia aenea dare volēbat.
sed perīculōsum erat quod Charisa parva erat.

6. postrīdiē omnēs ad vīllam reveniēbant. iterum crepundia dabant.

 WORDS TO HELP

Nouns

amīcī (m pl) friends
bullās (f pl) lockets
cognātī (m pl) relations
crepundia (n pl) rattles/toys
diēs (m) day
dōna (n pl) presents
gladius (m) sword
nōmen (n) name
vīlla (f) house

Verbs

amō I love
dabant they were giving
erās you (*sing*) were
erō I will be
gerēbant they were wearing
reveniēbant they were returning
spargēbat he was sprinkling
tenēbat he was holding
veniēbant they were coming

Infinitive
dare to give

Adjectives

aeneus/a/um made of bronze
duo/duae/duo two
ligneus/a/um made of wood
lūstricus/a/um of purification
meus/a/um my
octāvus/a/um eighth

Adverbs

fortasse perhaps
ōlim at some time
postrīdiē on the next day

GRASP THE GRAMMAR

The twins were born two months ago and they were named on the eighth and ninth days after their birth.

So Rufus and Lepidina had to use verbs in the **past** tense to describe the celebrations to Pandora.

They use the **imperfect** tense, which we met in the last chapter. Can you find the imperfect verbs in the first eight pictures? What does each one mean?

Verbs in the imperfect tense are easy to spot because they all include the letters **-ba-**. Remember that the ending of a Latin verb tells you *who* is doing the action.

But you won't be surprised to learn that the imperfect of the verb "to be" doesn't follow the pattern: it is **irregular**.

"To be" is a really important verb. Compare and learn the two tenses, **present** and **imperfect**.

Present tense	Imperfect tense
sum I am	**eram** I was
es you are (sing.)	**erās** you were (sing.)
est he/she/it is	**erat** he/she/it was
sumus we are	**erāmus** we were
estis you are (pl.)	**erātis** you were (pl.)
sunt they are	**erant** they were

Now look back at pictures 2, 4, 5, 9 and 10. Find the examples of the verb "to be" in the **imperfect** tense in each picture. What does each one mean?

LATIN ROOTS

Use your knowledge of Latin to explain the underlined word in each sentence.

1 Fran is an excellent musician and enjoys playing in her <u>octet</u>.
2 The teenagers were punished for their <u>infantile</u> behaviour.
3 The crocodile seized the man's leg in a <u>tenacious</u> grip.

ROMAN REPORT

Welcoming a baby

Shortly after the birth of a baby an important event took place, the **diēs lūstricus**: this was a day of purification for both mother and baby. It was also the occasion when the baby was named. It took place on the eighth day after birth for a girl and on the ninth for a boy. Friends and family would come to the baby's home to enjoy a celebratory meal. They would bring presents, such as toys and flowers. Especially popular were **crepundia**; these were small metal toys that would usually be tied around the baby's neck. The baby would enjoy the clinking noise that they made, just like a modern rattle.

On this special day, the baby was also given a **bulla**. This gold locket (or leather for a poorer family) contained charms to drive away evil spirits. A boy would not remove his **bulla** until he "put on the toga" when he became a man, at about the age of sixteen; a girl would not remove her **bulla** until her wedding day.

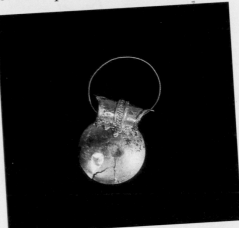

A child's **bulla**

Time to go home

After the naming ceremonies, Lepidina and the family returned to
their home in Eboracum. Flavius decided to follow on later, after a day's
hunting with a friend. Candidus is describing the hunt to Pandora.

maximus aper in silvīs erat.

Flāvius et Brocchus aprum petēbant, sed frūstrā.

tandem septem perdīcēs, quīnque leporēs et ūnus cervus mortuī erant.

diēs optimus erat.

ita vērō. Silvānus nōbīscum aderat.

 WORDS TO HELP

Nouns

aper (m) boar
canēs (m pl) dogs
cervus (m) deer
domus (f) home
leporēs (m pl) hares
perdīcēs (m pl) partridges
rētia (n pl) nets
segōsī (m pl) segosi (a breed of hunting dog)
silva (f) wood
Silvānus (m) god of hunting
vēnābula (n pl) hunting spears
vēnātiō (f) hunt
vertragī (m pl) vertragi (another breed of hunting dog)

Verbs

aderam I was there
discēdēbant they were leaving
faciēbās you were doing
olfaciēbant they were sniffing/smelling
petēbant they were searching for
portābam I was carrying
ululābant they were howling

Imperative
cūrā! take care of!

Adverbs

celerrimē very quickly
frūstrā in vain

Pronoun

hī these

Idiom

nōbīscum with us (**nōbīs** [pronoun] + **cum** [preposition])

GRASP THE GRAMMAR

Once again, the picture story was all in the past, so Candidus used the **imperfect** tense to tell it. Have another look at the picture story: there are 16 verbs in the **imperfect** tense.

Can you find them all? Remember to look for the **-ba-** in the verb!

And remember that the verb "to be" is irregular: it has a different set of endings for its imperfect tense.

A few other verbs follow the pattern of the verb "to be" and you have met one of them here: **adsum** (I am here or I am present). Find it in pictures 2, 4 and 10. Can you work out what it means each time?

When we take a simple verb like **sum** (I am) and add a **prefix** (a little word that goes in front of the verb), we make a brand-new verb. This kind of verb is called a **compound verb**.

The verb "to be" has several **compounds**. Here are some of them:

absum I am away   **praesum** I am in charge

adsum I am here   **subsum** I am under

īnsum I am in   **supersum** I survive

possum I am able

Here is some practice with compounds of the verb "to be". They're all in the imperfect tense. What does each one mean?

1 aderat	**6** ineram
2 suberāmus	**7** aderātis
3 poterant	**8** praeerat
4 supererāmus	**9** aberāmus
5 aberās	**10** poterat

 LATIN ROOTS

Use your knowledge of Latin to work out the meaning of the underlined words.

1 We took Blackie for training at the <u>canine</u> club.

2 The children behaved <u>amicably</u> towards the new pupil.

3 In geography we are finding out about our country's <u>imports</u> and <u>exports</u>.

4 A museum <u>curator</u> must make sure that no one steals precious objects.

5 I get so <u>frustrated</u> when I can't learn Latin vocabulary!

Hunting

We can read about Flavius's friend Brocchus in several of the letters from Vindolanda. Brocchus was the prefect of the nearby fort at Briga. In their spare time, Flavius and Brocchus loved to go hunting. In one letter Flavius asked Brocchus to send him some hunting nets "and you should repair the pieces very strongly".

Although York (Eboracum) is a big city today, when Flavius lived there it was a much smaller town surrounded by woods. Hunting was one of the main forms of relaxation for both soldiers and civilians. People hunted on horseback or on foot. They hunted all kinds of animals and they also liked to hunt birds, including geese and swans. Fishing was popular too. In Roman times, Britain was famous for producing excellent hunting dogs.

Corinthus was not interested in joining the hunt, but Candidus's description has reminded him of a famous Greek story about a boar. He tells the story to Candidus and Pandora.

THE HUNT FOR THE CALYDONIAN BOAR

Oeneus, King of Calydon, forgot to sacrifice to the goddess Artemis. Enraged, she sent a monstrous boar to ravage the countryside. Oeneus's son, Meleager, gathered together several Greek heroes and the beautiful huntress Atalanta, and they set off on a great boarhunt. Meleager fell in love with Atalanta, so he was delighted when she aimed her spear at the boar and was the first to draw blood. The boar went mad with pain and several of the heroes were killed, along with their hunting dogs. Finally Meleager struck the fatal blow. He presented Atalanta with the head and the hide of the boar, believing that she deserved the triumph. This caused great jealousy among the heroes and a fight broke out, which resulted in Meleager's tragic death.

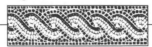

Barates comes to buy

WORDS TO HELP

Nouns

ātrium (n) hall
condiciōnēs (f pl) terms/agreement
ōrnātrīx (f) hairdresser

Adjectives

cārus/a/um expensive/dear
ducentōs two hundred
miser/a/um unhappy
sōlus/a/um alone/lonely

Verbs

festīnat he hurries
quaerit he looks for

Imperatives

parā! prepare!
quaere! look for!

Impersonal verb

placetne tibi? does it please you?/is it OK with you?

Infinitives

ēmere to buy

Participles

ducta led
ēmpta bought
iussus ordered
missus sent
vocātus called

Conjunction

igitur therefore

Idioms

ā dominō by his master
quam celerrimē as quickly as possible
quantī est? how much is she?

Exclamation

ehem! aha!

GRASP THE GRAMMAR

You have already learnt four different forms of verbs – **tenses**, **commands** (or imperatives), **infinitives** and **impersonal** verbs. Now for one more!

This new **part** of the verb is called a **participle**. A participle comes from a verb, so it is an action word, but it behaves like an **adjective**.

For example, in picture 4, Candidus is "**sent** by his master". The Latin word for "sent" is **missus**, the participle from the verb **mittere** (to send).

Compare this with picture 5: "Pandora, **led** into the hall . . ." The Latin word for "led" is **ducta**, the participle from the verb **dūcere** (to lead). Because Pandora is feminine, the word **ductus** has to have the feminine ending, **duct<u>a</u>**. We say that the participle must **agree** with the noun.

Find the participles in pictures 2, 8 and 9. Can you remember what each one means? Is each one masculine or feminine?

LATIN ROOTS

Use your knowledge of Latin to explain the underlined word in each sentence.

1 The secret agent was sent on a dangerous <u>mission</u>.
2 A teacher with a tidy desk? Now there's a <u>novelty</u>!
3 The Colosseum in Rome was the setting for many extraordinary <u>spectacles</u>.
4 Captured slaves were paraded through the streets of Rome; crowds lined the streets to taunt and <u>deride</u> them.
5 Pupils are often given an <u>induction</u> day when they start at a new school.

ROMAN REPORT

Barates

We originally met Barates in the first *Minimus* book. He is a real historical figure and we can find out many details of his life from his tombstone, which is in Corbridge; his wife Regina's tombstone is in South Shields. Barates was a **vexillārius**, or flag-maker. He bought Regina as a slave, then freed her and married her. Sadly, Regina died aged 30 but Barates lived until he was 68.

Barates came from Palmyra, in Syria at the far eastern edge of the Roman Empire; Regina was a Celtic girl. What language do you think they used to communicate with each other?

Slave girl wanted!

Lepidina is cross when she discovers that Flavius has sold Pandora.

 ## WORDS TO HELP

Nouns

catēnīs (f pl) chains
ēdicta (n pl) placards
mercātus (m) market
pretium (n) price
tribūnal (n) platform
vēnālīcius (m) slave-dealer
vīta (f) life

Verbs

cōnstituunt they agree
dēbēmus we must
gerunt they wear
redeunt they return
scit she knows

Participles
positās positioned/placed
trādita handed over
vīnctōs tied up

Adverbs

satis! enough
timidē nervously/timidly

Adjectives

Hispānicus/a/um Spanish
melior better
novus/a/um new

N.B. The name **Trifōsa** means "delicious"!

GRASP THE GRAMMAR

> Can you find the **participle** in picture 2?

Now look at the noun it is describing and look closely at the endings of both the **noun** and the **participle**.

The slaves are described by the **participle**: **vīnctōs** (tied up). The participle has to be masculine and plural, because the slaves are masculine and plural.

Remember, a participle must be the same number, gender and case as the noun it is describing.

> Now look at pictures 3, 5 and 9. In each case, find the **participle** and then the **noun that it is describing.**

Candidus says that choosing between slave girls must be rather like the beauty contest in which Paris had to judge between three goddesses. He tells Trifosa the story.

THE BEAUTY CONTEST

The goddess of strife, Eris, came uninvited to a wedding feast and caused trouble by bringing with her a golden apple. On this apple were engraved, in Greek, the words "To the fairest". Three goddesses, Hera, Athene and Aphrodite, each hoped to be awarded this prize. Zeus, the king of the gods, was reluctant to make the decision himself and asked the Trojan prince, Paris, to be the judge of the competition. The messenger god, Hermes, took the three goddesses to Mount Ida near Troy and told Paris to choose the most beautiful. Each of the three goddesses tried to bribe him. Hera offered Paris power and wealth, Athene offered wisdom and military victories while Aphrodite offered him the most beautiful woman in the world, Helen of Sparta. Paris gave the apple to Aphrodite and went to Sparta to claim his prize. He abducted Helen (who was already married to a Greek king) and they sailed off to Troy. This sparked off the Trojan wars, and it explains why Helen's face is known as "the face that launched a thousand ships".

The new headquarters

Rufus and Flavius are walking around Eboracum. Everyone seems to be involved with the new building projects.

7 ecce! sculptōrēs columnās sculpunt.

8 sed operāriī cessant. īgnavī sunt! cervesiam bibunt!

9 dīligenter labōrāte!

10 operāriī, ā Flāviō iussī, invītī labōrāre incipiunt.

 ## WORDS TO HELP

Nouns

aedificium (n) building

agrimēnsōrēs (m pl) surveyors

cervesia (f) beer

dēsignātiō (f) plan

grōma (f) groma (surveying instrument)

lapicīdīnae (f pl) quarry

operāriī (m pl) labourers

prīncipia (n pl) headquarters

saccāriī (m pl) dockers

terra (f) ground

Verbs

cessant they stop

complānant they level

cōnfirmant they check

dēsignāmus we design

incipiunt they begin

īnspiciunt they inspect

sculpunt they carve

tollunt they lift

Participles

iussī ordered

secta cut

tracta dragged

Adjectives

īgnavus/a/um lazy

invītus/a/um unwilling

GRASP THE GRAMMAR

Once again, look carefully at all the verbs. What **parts** of the verb can you recognise?

There are three more **participles**, in pictures 1, 2 and 10.

Find them and remind yourself of what each one means. Can you see which noun they agree with?

If you look carefully you will also find one example of an infinitive and one imperative. Find them and translate them.

LATIN ROOTS

Use your knowledge of Latin to explain the underlined word in each sentence.

1 We spent our biology lesson <u>dissecting</u> frogs.
2 If you work <u>diligently</u> you can expect to do well in the examinations.
3 Talking to yourself is said to be a sign of <u>incipient</u> madness.
4 Why did the ancient world give the name <u>Mediterranean</u> to that sea? (Clue: **medius** means "middle" in Latin.)

ROMAN REPORT

Construction work at Eboracum

The first fortress at Eboracum was constructed of timber. It was built by the legionary soldiers who arrived in AD 72. In the early years of the second century AD, the decision was made to replace it with a stone building. Building in stone was still quite unusual and the local Celtic people would have viewed the construction work with amazement and possibly with some alarm. As well as making a more permanent and comfortable base for themselves, the Roman soldiers were giving a clear message that they were here to stay.

This major period of building activity would have required tons of stone. The stone was brought to Eboracum from the Pennines and was transported along the River Ouse by barge and then by cart to the building sites.

The most important building was the military headquarters, or **prīncipia**. It was built on the site of the present York Minster and was probably just as imposing. You can still see the foundations of the building in the undercroft of the Minster. It was massive and would have required a huge number of builders, surveyors, sculptors and general labourers. The building work would have caused great interest and excitement in Eboracum.

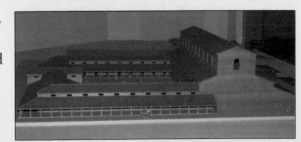

Model from the undercroft, York Minster

Some builders are better than others . . .

Flavius is supervising another group of soldiers who are constructing a stone gateway. Rufus enjoys watching them.

1. castellum ligneum dēlētum est. nunc aliī mīlitēs castellum lapideum aedificant.

2. castellum solidum est.
   omnēs Brigantēs attonitī stant.

3. aliī mīlitēs portam maximam aedificant.

4. mīlitēs dēscrīptiōnem habent, in tabulā pictam.

5. sculptor optimus, ā Flāviō iussus, īnscrīptiōnem sculpere incipit.

6. mīlitēs saxa maxima tollunt. Brigantēs polyspaston mīrābile spectant.

 WORDS TO HELP

Nouns

Brigantēs (m pl) members of a British tribe
castellum (n) fortress
dēscrīptiō (f) drawing
fragor (m) crash
locō (m) place
polyspaston (n) crane
porta (f) gate

Verbs

habent they have
omittunt they drop
servat he saves
stant they stand
tollunt they lift

Participles
dēlētum destroyed
percussus struck
pictam drawn

Imperative
cavēte! watch out!

Adjectives

attonitus/a/um astonished
ingēns huge
lapideus/a/um made of stone
ligneus/a/um made of wood
mīrābile amazing
propriō correct
vīvus/a/um alive

Adverb

paene almost

GRASP THE GRAMMAR

There are four more **participles** for you to find in the picture story. Remember that participles behave like **adjectives**, so they must have the same **gender** as the noun they are describing. Two of the participles in the picture story are masculine, one is feminine and one is neuter. Can you work out which is which?

LATIN ROOTS

1 Why are the <u>percussion</u> instruments in an orchestra given that name?

2 What do you think a <u>lapidary</u> works with?

3 "Westminster Abbey is a magnificent <u>edifice</u>." Explain this sentence using a simpler word.

4 The <u>Picts</u> were a tribe from northern Britain who were heavily tattooed. How did they get their name?

ROMAN REPORT

An inscription

Above the gate that the soldiers are constructing in this story was an inscription, honouring the emperor Trajan. It records the construction of the gate in AD 107 by the Ninth Legion. Enough of the inscription remains for us to complete the missing letters.

In the bottom line you can see that the gate was built by the Ninth Legion, from Spain (HISP.). LEG is short for **legiō** (legion) and it is followed by VIIII, another form of the Roman numerals for the number nine (IX).

Rufus returns home with the frightened mouse. She soon makes friends with Minimus, and Rufus names her "Minima". Rufus explains to Corinthus how Minima was almost crushed by the falling stone. Corinthus tells Rufus that the famous Greek hero Odysseus was nearly killed by a huge boulder too . . .

NEVER SHOW OFF TO A GIANT

Once upon a time the great Greek hero Odysseus found himself trapped, with twelve of his men, inside the cave of Polyphemus, the Cyclops. Trying to persuade the one-eyed giant to stop eating his men, Odysseus introduced himself as Nobody and offered the giant some wine. Once the giant was drunk, Odysseus blinded him and he and his surviving men escaped to the safety of their ship. Polyphemus cried out to the other Cyclops that Nobody had hurt him. So they would not come to help him, and he had to stumble and grope his way to the seashore in pursuit of the Greeks.

As he sailed away, Odysseus boasted to the Cyclops, revealing his true identity: "If anyone asks you how you came by your blindness, tell him your eye was put out by Odysseus, sacker of cities, son of Laertes, who lives in Ithaca."

Polyphemus was so enraged that he prayed to his father Poseidon to give Odysseus a troublesome journey home across the ocean. Then he hurled a massive boulder at Odysseus's ship, and almost caused it to sink.

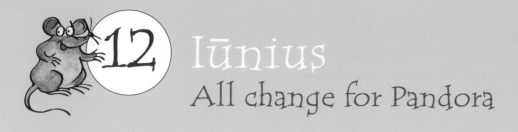
Freedom!

1. intrāte! exspectātissimī estis!

   Barātes familiam ad cēnam invītat.

2. mihi placet Pandōram līberāre. Pandōra! sedē mēcum!

3. volō vōs testēs esse. Pandōram līberō.

   ita vērō. euge!

4. Pandōra, līberta facta, laetissima est.

5. Trifōsa! Pandōra nunc līberta est. necesse est tibi cibum offerre.

6. Trifōsa cibum timidē importat.

WORDS TO HELP

Nouns
līberta (f) freedwoman
squālor (m) mess
testēs (m pl) witnesses

Adverb
ubīque everywhere

Verbs
adiuvant they help
edunt they eat
eris you (*sing*) will be
importat she carries in

Infinitives
esse to be
līberāre to set free

Participle
facta made

REVISE THE GRAMMAR

Look at the picture story again. Try to spot the following points of grammar – you've met them all in this book!

3 personal pronouns	4 infinitives
1 singular imperative	1 participle
1 plural imperative	1 compound verb
1 negative imperative	1 imperfect tense
2 impersonal verbs	

Write them all down in Latin and label them; then translate them.

LATIN ROOTS

Use your knowledge of Latin to work out the meaning of the underlined word in each sentence.

1 I bought that fruit last week so I'm not sure if it's still <u>edible</u>.
2 I saw the car accident so I may need to <u>testify</u> in court.
3 Your bedroom is utterly <u>squalid</u>! Please tidy it up at once.
4 Many soldiers lost their lives in the war, fighting for <u>liberty</u>.

ROMAN REPORT

Freeing slaves

In the Roman world, not all masters were cruel. Many decided to free their slaves and this act was called **manumission**. The word literally means "sending from the hand", from **mittere** (to send) and **manus** (hand). Slaves could be given their freedom in a number of ways: a master might summon witnesses to a special ceremony, where the slave wore the **pilleus** (cap of freedom) and was touched on the shoulder with a rod. The slave then became a **lībertus** (freedman) or **līberta** (freedwoman). Alternatively a master might give freedom to his slaves in his will, or he might do it more informally by simply inviting a slave to join him at dinner, as Barates does in our story. The presence of the family as witnesses is important: it makes the event legal.

The party continues

Trifōsa optimē saltat.
Corinthus et Candidus rīdent.

sed Vibrissa dormit.

 WORDS TO HELP

Nouns	Verbs
flābellum (n) fan	**celebrēmus** let us celebrate!/let's party!
spōnsa (f) fiancée	**ērubēscit** she blushes
spōnsus (m) fiancé	**pōnit** she puts
uxor (f) wife	**trādit** he hands over

Adjectives	Adverb
alius/a/um other, another	**statim** immediately
fēlīx lucky	
tertius/a/um third	

LATIN ROOTS

1 Latin is a great help with learning modern languages.

The phrase **grātiās agō** means "I thank" and leads to the English words "grateful" and "gratitude".

Can you find out how to say "thank you" in Italian and Spanish?

2 The Latin for "ring" is **ānulus**. The Romans used the same finger for wedding and engagement rings as people usually do today. Try to find out what French people call this finger; it is linked to the Latin word.

ROMAN REPORT

Betrothal

Slaves could not marry so Barates had to free Pandora in order to make her his wife. In this story they celebrate the **spōnsālia**, or betrothal ceremony. These ceremonies were very common and sometimes took place when the engaged couple were still young children. There was no legal minimum age.

Friends and relatives would gather for a celebratory dinner and some of them would act as witnesses. Presents would be exchanged and the woman would wear a betrothal ring. In most parts of Europe these rings were made of bronze though iron rings were used in Germany.

When Barates announces that he wants to marry Pandora, she says, "How lucky I am!" Do you agree with her?

A betrothal ring

This is the sort of fan that Barates gives to Pandora

After the betrothal party, everyone is tired but very happy.
They are looking forward to the wedding. As usual, Corinthus
has a story to fit the occasion.

THE MARRIAGE OF PELEUS AND THETIS

Peleus was a brave Greek and a great favourite of the centaur Cheiron, who
taught many heroes at his home on Mount Pelion. Peleus had fallen in love with
the elusive sea-goddess Thetis, and Cheiron advised him how he could win her
as a bride.

Peleus made his way to a lonely sea-shore and crouched by the water's edge,
hidden near the mouth of a dark cave. Thetis came skimming over the waves on
the back of a dolphin, and entered the cave to sleep through the heat of the day.
Peleus seized her in his arms and clung tightly as the infuriated goddess
changed from shape to shape, trying to throw off her captor. She turned herself
into fire, burning Peleus's hands, and then into water that nearly slipped
through his clutching fingers. She became a fierce lion, a hissing serpent and a
deadly, throttling cuttlefish, but Peleus refused to let go.

Finally, impressed by his determination, Thetis consented to marry him. They
were married on Mount Pelion, and the wedding was attended by all the gods
and goddesses.

Glossary

Verbs: the alternative ending is for the infinitive (e.g. **accipere** to welcome)

Adjectives: the alternative endings are for the masculine, feminine and neuter forms

A

ā/ab by, from
absum, -esse I am absent, away
accipiō, -ere I welcome, receive
ad to, towards
adiuvō, -āre I help
adsum, -esse I am present, here
adveniō, -īre I arrive
advesperāscit it is becoming dark
aedificium (n) building
aedificō, -āre I build
aeneus, -a, -um bronze
agitātus, -a, -um excited
agrimēnsor (m) surveyor
aliī . . . aliī some . . . others
alius another
alter, -era, -erum the other (of two)
ambulō, -āre I walk
amīcus (m) friend
amō, -āre I love
amphora (f) jar
ancilla (f) slave girl
animal (n) animal
annus (m) year
ante before
ānulus (m) ring
anxius, -a, -um anxious
aper (m) boar
appropinquō, -āre I approach
aqua (f) water
arcessō, -ere I summon
architectus (m) architect
ardeō, -ēre I burn
arma (n pl) weapons
ascendō, -ere I climb up
astrologus (m) astrologer
ātrium (n) hall
attonitus, -a, -um astonished

audiō, -īre I hear, listen
avia (f) grandmother
avunculus (m) uncle
avus (m) grandfather

B

bellum (n) war
benignus, -a, -um kind
bibō, -ere I drink
bonus, -a, -um good
Brigantēs (m pl) a British tribe
bulla (f) locket

C

Calēdonia (f) Scotland
calidus, -a, -um hot
candēla (f) candle
canis (m *or* f) dog
cantō, -āre I sing
capiō, -ere I take
capra (f) she-goat
cārissimus, -a, -um dearest
cārus, -a, -um dear, expensive
castellum (n) fortress
Cataractōnium (n) Catterick
catēna (f) chain
cavē/cavēte! be careful! watch out!
celebrō, -āre I celebrate, party
celeriter quickly
celerrimē very quickly
cēna (f) dinner
cēnō, -āre I dine
cervesia (f) beer
cervus (m) deer
cessō, -āre I stop, cease
cibus (m) food
circum round

clāmor (m)   noise/shouting
clārus, -a, -um   famous
clāvus (m)   nail
cognātī (m pl)   relations
colligō, -ere   I collect
columna (f)   column
complānō, -āre   I level, flatten
condiciōnēs (f pl)   terms, agreement
condō, -ere   I store
cōnfirmō, -āre   I check
cōnstituō, -ere   I agree
cōnstruō, -ere   I build
cōnsulō, -ere   I consult
cōnsūmō, -ere   I eat
coquō, -ere   I cook
cotīdiē   every day
crepundia (n pl)   toys, rattles
cubiculum (n)   bedroom
cum   with
cūr?   why?
cūrō, -āre   I look after
currō, -ere   I run
currus (m)   chariot
custōdiō, -īre   I guard

D

Dācia (f)   Dacia
Dānuvius (m)   River Danube
dea (f)   goddess
deae mātrēs (f pl)   mother goddesses
dēbeō, -ēre   I must
dēcidō, -ere   I fall
dēfendō, -ere   I defend
dēleō, -ēre   I destroy
dēlētus, -a, -um   destroyed
Delphī (m pl)   Delphi
Delphicus, -a, -um   Delphic
dēmōnstrō, -āre   I show
dēnārius (m)   (Roman silver) coin
dēscendō, -ere   I climb down
dēscrīptiō (f)   drawing
dēsignātiō (f)   plan
dēsignō, -āre   I design, plan
dētergeō, -ēre   I clean up
dētrahō, -ere   I remove
deus (m)   god
dīcō, -ere   I say
diēs (m or f)   day
difficile (est)   (it is) difficult
digitus (m)   finger
dīligēns   hard-working
dīligenter   carefully
discēdō, -ere   I leave

discō, -ere   I learn
diū   for a long time
dō, -āre   I give
doleō, -ēre   I am in pain
dominus (m)   master
domus (f)   home, house
dōnō, -āre   I present, donate
dōnum (n)   present, gift
dormiō, -īre   I sleep
ducentī   two hundred
ductus, -a, -um   led
duo   two
dux (m)   leader

E

ē/ex   from, out of
Eborācum (n)   York
ecce!   look!
ēdicta (n pl)   placards
edō, -ere   I eat
efflō, -āre   I blow
ego   I
ehem!   aha!, hm!, well!
ēheu!   alas!, oh no!
ēmō, -ere   I buy
ēmptus, -a, -um   bought
epistula (f)   letter
equitō, -āre   I ride
equus (m)   horse
eram   I was
erat   he/she was
erit   he/she will be
erō   I will be
ērubēscō, -ere   I blush
esse   to be
et   and
euge!   hooray!
ex/ē   from, out of
exeō, -īre   I go out
explicō, -āre   I explain
exspectātissimus, -a, -um   very welcome

F

faber (m)   workman
fābula (f)   story
facile (est)   (it is) easy
faciō, -ere   I make, do
factus, -a, -um   made, done
familia (f)   family, household
fēlīx   lucky
ferrārius (m)   blacksmith
fessus, -a, -um   tired
festīnō, -āre   I hurry

figlīna (f)   pottery workshop
figulus (m)   potter
fīlia (f)   daughter
fīlius (m)   son
flābellum (n)   fan
flamma (f)   flame
flūmen (n)   river
foedus, -a, -um   disgusting
fornāx (f)   forge
fortasse   perhaps
fortis, -is, -e   brave
fortiter   bravely
Fortūna (f)   Fortune
fossa (f)   ditch
fragor (m)   crash
frīgidus, -a, -um   cold
frondēs (f pl)   leaves, herbs
frūmentum (n)   grain
frūstrā   in vain
fundō, -ere   I pour

G

Gallia (f)   Gaul
geminī (m pl)   twins
Germānia (f)   Germany
Germānicus, -a, -um   German
gerō, -ere   I wage; wear
gladius (m)   sword
Graecia (f)   Greece
Graecus, -a, -um   Greek
grammaticus (m)   teacher
grātiās agō, -ere   I thank
grātulātiōnēs (f pl)   congratulations
gravidus, -a, -um   heavy; pregnant
grōma (f)   surveying instrument
gustō, -āre   I taste

H

habeō, -ēre   I have
habitō, -āre   I live (in)
hās   these
hī   these
hic, haec, hoc   this
hilariter   cheerfully
Hispānicus, -a, -um   Spanish
hodiē   today
honestus, -a, -um   honourable, virtuous
horoscopus (m)   horoscope
horreum (n)   granary
hūc   to here
hūc . . . illūc   here and there, up and down

I

iactō, -āre   I throw, toss
ibi   there
igitur   therefore
īgnavus, -a, -um   lazy
imperātor (m)   emperor
importō, -āre   I carry in
in   in, on, into
incēdō, -ere   I march
incipiō, -ere   I begin, start
īnfāns (m or f)   baby
ingēns   huge
īnscrīptiō (f)   inscription
īnspiciō, -ere   I inspect
īnsum, -esse   I am in
intentē   closely
intereā   meanwhile
intrō, -āre   I come in, enter
inveniō, -īre   I find
invītō, -āre   I invite
invītus, -a, -um   unwilling
involvō, -ere   I wrap up
iocōsē   playfully
iocus (m)   joke
īta vērō!   yes!
Italia (f)   Italy
iter (n)   journey
iterum   again
iūcundus, -a, -um   lovely
iussus, -a, -um   ordered, told
iuvenis (m)   young man

L

labōrō, -āre   I work
lacrimō, -āre   I cry, weep
laetissimus, -a, -um   very happy
laetus, -a, -um   happy
lapicīdīnae (f pl)   quarry
lapideus, -a, -um   made of stone
Larēs (m pl)   household gods
lāridum (n)   lard
Latīnus, -a, -um   Latin
lavō, -āre   I wash
lectīca (f)   litter (sedan-chair)
lectus (m)   couch
legiōnēs (f pl)   legions
legō, -ere   I read
lēniter   gently
lentē   slowly
lepus (m)   hare
liber (m)   book
līberō, -āre   I set free
līberta (f)   freedwoman

(tibi) licet   (you) may
ligneus, -a, -um   made of wood
lignum (n)   log, beam, plank
līmōsus, -a, -um   muddy
lingua (f)   tongue; language
litterae (f pl)   letters
locus (m)   place
longus, -a, -um   long
lūbricus, -a, -um   slippery
lūstricus, -a, -um   of purification

M

māchina (f)   machine
magnificus, -a, -um   magnificent
malus, -a, -um   bad
mandō, -ere   I chew
maneō, -ēre   I wait, stay
mare (n)   sea
marītus (m)   husband
māter (f)   mother
maximē   very strongly
maximus, -a, -um   very big
mēcum   with me
melior   better
mercātus (m)   market
meus, -a, -um   my
mihi   for me
mīles (m)   soldier
mīlia   thousands
mīlitēs (m pl)   soldiers
minimē!   no! not at all!
mīrābilis   marvellous, amazing
mīrāculum (n)   marvel, miracle
mīrus, -a, -um   wonderful
miser, -a, -um   unhappy
missus, -a, -um   sent
modicus, -a, -um   ordinary
mortuus, -a, -um   dead
mulceō, -ēre   I stroke
multī, -ae, -a   many
murmurō, -āre   purr
mūs (m *or* f)   mouse

N

nam   for
nātus, -a, -um   born
nauta (m)   sailor
nāvigō, -āre   I sail
nāvis (f)   ship
necessārius, -a, -um   necessary
necesse (est/erit)   (it is/will be) necessary
nescio, -īre   I do not know
nihil   nothing

ningit   it is snowing
nōbīs   for/to us
nōbīscum   with us
nōlī, nōlīte!   don't!
nōmen (n)   name
nōmine   by name
nōn   not
nōnne?   surely?
noster, -ra, -um   our
nōtissimus, -a, -um   very famous
nōtus, -a, -um   famous
novus, -a, -um   new
nunc   now
nūper   recently

O

obēsus, -a, -um   fat
obstetrīx (f)   midwife
octāvus, -a, -um   eighth
offerō, -rre   I bring out
officīna (f)   workshop
olfaciō, -ere   I sniff, smell
ōlim   at some time, once upon a time
ōlla (f)   pot
omittō, -ere   I drop
omnēs   everyone
operārius (m)   labourer
optimē   very well
optimus, -a, -um   the best, excellent
ōrāculum (n)   oracle
ōrnātrīx (f)   hairdresser
ōrō, -āre   I pray

P

paene   almost
parō, -āre   I prepare
parvus, -a, -um   small
pater (m)   father
patera (f)   bowl
paucī, -ae, -a   few
pāvō (m)   peacock
percussus, -a, -um   struck
perdīx (m *or* f)   partridge
perīculōsus, -a, -um   dangerous
perītē   skilfully
perterritus, -a, -um   terrified
petō, -ere   I search for, seek
phalerae (f pl)   decorations, medals
pictus, -a, -um   drawn, depicted
pila (f)   ball
pilleus (m)   cap of freedom
pīpiō, -āre   I chirp
(mihi) placet   it pleases (me), I would like